YOUR GUIDE
to the world's most
DOOFY BIRDS

COLORING BOOK

Created by
Dana Wheeles

ISBN: 978-1-7366015-2-5

See also

Your Guide to the World's Most Doofy Birds (2021)

The Magical Journey: A Tale of Beauty Lost and Found (2020)

www.danawheeles.com
www.deerhawkhealing.com

COASTAL

Colors in the Wild →

- Black
- White
- Orange
- Red

Where do they live? Color in the range map below.

Atlantic Puffin live throughout the North Atlantic Ocean and can be seen during breeding season on cliffs in Newfoundland, Greenland, Iceland and Ireland.

ATLANTIC PUFFIN
Fratercula arctica

Colors in the Wild →

- Blue
- White
- Brown

Where do they live? Color in the range map below.

Blue-footed Boobies are best known for being found on the Galapagos Islands, but they range all along the Pacific Coast of the Americas, from California to Chile.

BLUE-FOOTED BOOBY
Sula nebouxii

Colors in the Wild →

- Black
- White
- Orange

Where do they live? Color in the range map below.

Inca Terns live along the rocky Pacific shores of Central and South America, from Nicaragua to Chile.

INCA TERN
Larosterna inca

Colors in the Wild →

- Black
- Red

Where do they live? Color in the range map below.

Magnificent Frigatebirds are abundant throughout the tropical and sub-tropical regions of the Western Hemisphere, notably in the Gulf of Mexico and the Pacific Coast of Central America.

Magnificent Frigatebird
Fregata magnificens

Colors in the Wild →

- Brown
- White
- Yellow

Where do they live? Color in the range map below.

Brown Pelicans are a familiar sight anywhere on the coast of North America and even the northernmost coasts of South America.

Brown Pelican

Pelecanus occidentalis

Colors in the Wild →

- Yellow-Brown
- Reddish-Brown
- Red
- Blue
- Black

Where do they live? Color in the range map below.

There are several species of flycatcher in South America, but the Royal Atlantic Flycatcher is only found in the forests of Eastern Brazil.

ATLANTIC ROYAL FLYCATCHER

Onychorhynchus coronatus swainsoni

Colors in the Wild →

· Black
· Blue
· Red
· White

Where do they live? Color in the range map below.

Bulwer's Pheasants are very rare, and can only be found in the wild on the island of Borneo in Southeast Asia.

BULWER'S PHEASANT

Lophura bulweri

Colors in the Wild →

- Brown
- Gray
- Black
- Yellow

Where do they live? Color in the range map below.

Common Potoo like open woodlands and grasslands all across South America, from Nicaragua to Uruguay.

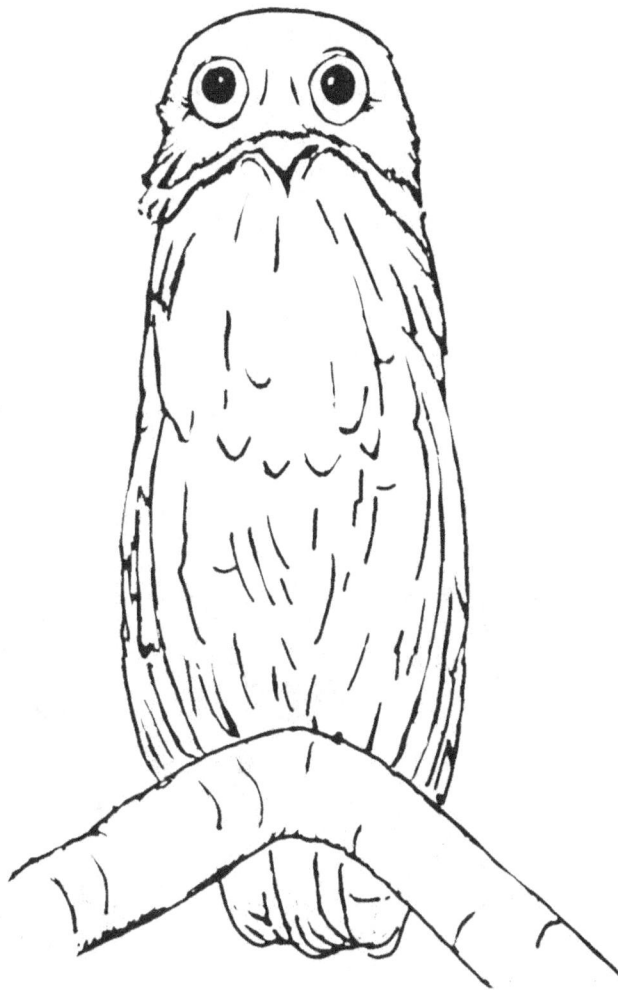

COMMON POTOO

Nyctibius griseus

Colors in the Wild →

- Black
- Brown
- Red
- Yellow
- White

Where do they live? Color in the range map below.

Helmeted Hornbills are native to the Malay Peninsula and other islands of Southeast Asia, such as Borneo and Sumatra.

HELMETED HORNBILL

Rhinoplax vigil

Colors in the Wild →

- Black
- Yellow
- Lime Green
- Orange
- Light Blue
- Red

Where do they live? Color in the range map below.

Keel-billed Toucans are a Central American species, living in forests from Mexico to Colombia. It is the national bird of Belize.

KEEL-BILLED TOUCAN

Ramphastos sulfuratus

Colors in the Wild →

- White
- Black
- Purple
- Blue
- Orange
- Red

Where do they live? Color in the range map below.

King Vultures are plentiful throughout Central and South America, from Mexico to Argentina.

KING VULTURE
Sarcoramphus papa

Colors in the Wild →

· Charcoal Gray
· Brown

Where do they live? Color in the range map below.

There are several sub-species of kiwi birds, all native to New Zealand. The Great Spotted Kiwi is the largest, and lives on the South Island.

KIWI BIRD
Apteryx haastii

Colors in the Wild →

· Black

Where do they live? Color in the range map below.

Long-wattled Umbrellabirds are endemic to the forests of
Ecuador and Colombia.

LONG-WATTLED UMBRELLABIRD

Cephalopterus penduliger

Colors in the Wild →

· Black
· White
· Orange
· Red

Where do they live? Color in the range map below.

Rhinoceros Hornbills are the national bird of Malaysia, and can also be found in the rainforests of Sumatra and Borneo.

RHINOCEROS HORNBILL

Buceros rhinoceros

Colors in the Wild →

· Black
· Blue
· Brown
· Red

Where do they live? Color in the range map below.

Southern Cassowaries are large flightless birds seen in the rainforests of Northeastern Australia and Papua New Guinea.

SOUTHERN CASSOWARY

Casuarius casuarius

GRASSLANDS

Colors in the Wild →

- Gray
- Black
- White
- Yellow
- Orange
- Pink

Where do they live? Color in the range map below.

Greater Sage-Grouse live in the meadows and highlands of western North America, including Wyoming, Montana, and the Canadian provinces of Alberta and Saskatchewan.

GREATER SAGE-GROUSE

Centrocercus urophasianus

Colors in the Wild →

- Brown
- Black
- White
- Yellow

Where do they live? Color in the range map below.

Kori Bustards can be seen throughout southern Africa,
especially in the countries of Botswana and Namibia.

Kori Bustard

Ardeotis kori

Colors in the Wild ➔

- Gray
- Black
- White
- Yellow
- Orange

Where do they live? Color in the range map below.

Secretary Birds live in the dry grasslands of southern Africa, throughout Kenya and Tanzania, and as far south as the country of South Africa.

SECRETARY BIRD

Sagittarius serpentarius

Colors in the Wild →

- Gray
- Dark Brown
- Black
- Yellow

Where do they live? Color in the range map below.

Tawny Frogmouths don't really have a preference when it comes to habitat: they are found in suburbs and woodlands, heaths and savannas. They are abundant throughout the Australian mainland and northern Tasmania.

TAWNY FROGMOUTH

Podargus strigoides

Colors in the Wild   →

- Black
- Blue
- White
- Red

Where do they live? Color in the range map below.

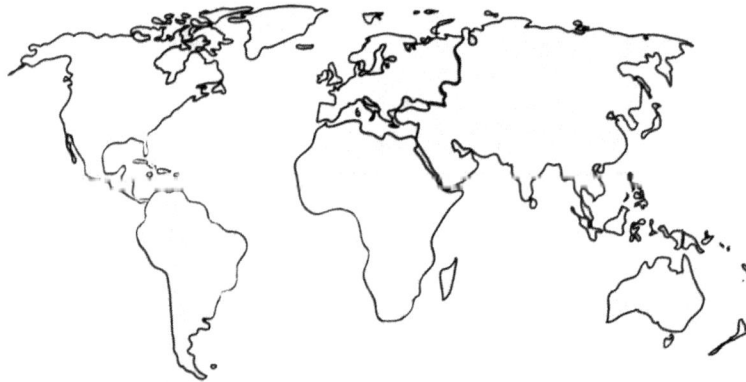

Vulturine Guineafowl are plentiful in the scrublands of
northeastern Africa, primarily in the countries of Ethiopia,
Kenya, and Tanzania.

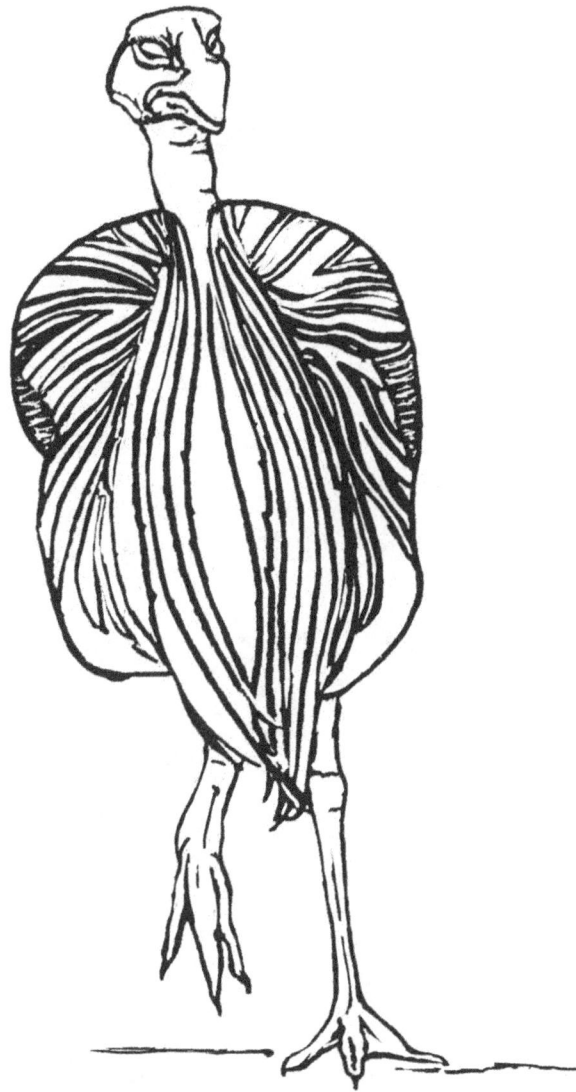

Vulturine Guineafowl

Acryllium vulturinum

Colors in the Wild →

· Brown
· Blue
· Red
· Black

Where do they live? Color in the range map below.

Wild Turkey can be seen in both grasslands and woodlands throughout North America, from Canada to southern Mexico.

WILD TURKEY
Meleagris gallopavo

WETLANDS

Colors in the Wild →

- Reddish Brown
- Light Blue
- Black
- White

Where do they live? Color in the range map below.

African Jacanas can be found throughout sub-Saharan Africa, including the countries of Ethiopia, Tanzania, Namibia, and Nigeria (among others).

African Jacana

Actophilornis africanus

Colors in the Wild →

- Dark Pink
- Light Pink
- Black
- White

Where do they live? Color in the range map below.

American Flamingoes can be found on and around
Caribbean islands, Caribbean Mexico, southern Florida,
Belize, coastal Colombia, northern Brazil, Venezuela and
Galápagos Islands.

AMERICAN FLAMINGO

Phoenicopterus ruber

Colors in the Wild →

- Orange-Brown
- Slate Blue
- Black
- White

Where do they live? Color in the range map below.

Bearded Reedlings have a large range across Europe to Asia. They can be found from reedbeds in England and all the way east to coastal China.

BEARDED REEDLING

Panurus biarmicus

Colors in the Wild →

- Light Pink
- Dark Pink
- White
- Yellow

Where do they live? Color in the range map below.

Roseate Spoonbills live in warm regions of the Americas, from the Gulf Coast of the United States to northern Argentina.

JABIRU

Jabiru mycteria

Colors in the Wild →

- Light Pink
- Dark Pink
- White
- Yellow

Where do they live? Color in the range map below.

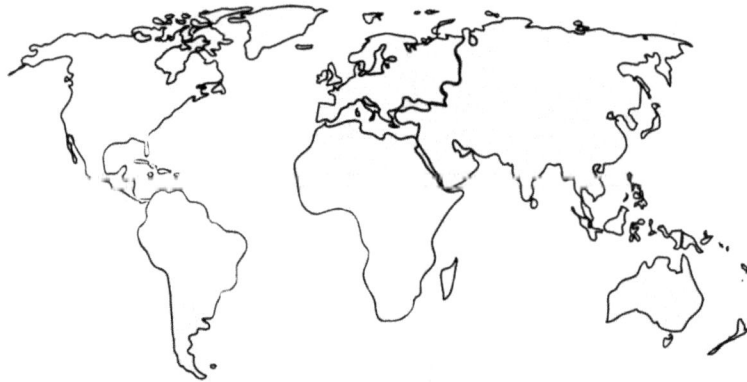

Roseate Spoonbills live in warm regions of the Americas, from the Gulf Coast of the United States to northern Argentina.

ROSEATE SPOONBILL

Platalea ajaja

Colors in the Wild →

- Blue
- Light Gray
- White
- Light Yellow

Where do they live? Color in the range map below.

Shoebills have a limited range of freshwater swamps in Africa. Sightings are particularly frequent in South Sudan, Congo, and Uganda.

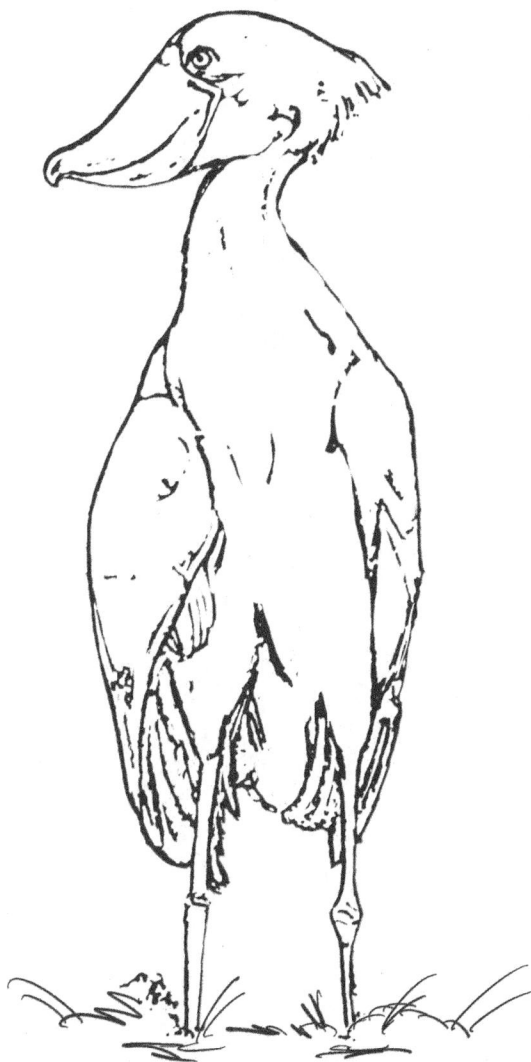

SHOEBILL STORK

Balaeniceps rex

Colors in the Wild →

· White
· Black
· Pink

Where do they live? Color in the range map below.

Wood Storks have a range through the Americas that overlaps with that of the Roseate Spoonbill. They can be seen as far north as coastal Georgia, and down south to Argentina.

WOOD STORK

Mycteria americana

Want to learn more about the Doofy Birds?

The information in this book came primarily from the online resources below. Visit these websites to learn more and see the doofs come to life.

- **ebird.org** (The Cornell Lab of Ornithology)
- **allaboutbirds.org** (The Cornell Lab of Ornithology)
- **en.wikipedia.org** (Wikimedia Foundation)

I've collected some of my favorite photos and videos on my own website for insiders like you. Scan the QR code below to get access.

SCAN ME

www.ingramcontent.com/pod-product-compliance
Lightning Source LLC
LaVergne TN
LVHW061340060426

835511LV00014B/2027